America's Ten Greatest Domestic Fears

Water Shortages, Epidemics and Disease, Domestic
Terrorism, Civil War, and More

DEREK G. AMERICA

America's 10 Greatest Domestic Fears
Copyright © 2014, 2016 Derek G. America, DGA Media.

Although the author and publisher have made every reasonable attempt to achieve complete accuracy of the content in this guide, they assume no responsibility for errors or omissions. Also, you should use this information as you see fit, and at your own risk. Your particular situation may not be exactly suited to the examples illustrated here; in fact, it's likely that they won't be the same, and you should adjust your use of the information and recommendations accordingly.

Any trademarks, service marks, product names, or named features are assumed to be the property of their respective owners, and are used only for reference. There is no implied endorsement if we use one of these terms. Finally, use your own judgement. Nothing in this ebook/guide is intended to replace common sense, legal, or any other professional advice, and is meant only to inform and entertain the reader.

The author greatly appreciates you taking the time to read his work. Please leave a review wherever you bought the book.

Thank you for supporting my work.
First Edition, v.1.6
Published by DGA Media

For my sweet wife and our little girl:
I truly want the world to be a great place for both of you.

Table of Contents

America's
Ten Greatest
Domestic Fears

Introduction

Last year while watching an episode of streaming TV, my wife got very nervous and asked if we would be prepared if things in our life changed — especially if they changed in a very big way. I think that's what good story-telling is supposed to do. It should make all of us think beyond the story, and question our feelings, motives, fears, and our own lives.

We were actually watching "Revolution," a post-apocalyptic science fiction story that imagines what the United States might be like if all of the electric power went out, and then never came back on. In their version, cities fell, governments collapsed, and the country eventually broke up into warring factions as various leaders tried to grab control of a seemingly simpler country.

But without electricity - technology, the internet, TV, radio, communication, travel, and more, lots more had to immediately change. The way we do so many things in our society and our entire culture is connected to electricity, so it was a pretty creative idea to imagine what it would be like if it all was gone.

No more laptop, no more cars, no more planes, no cell phones, no internet, no Facebook...

But it wasn't a passing concern for her... She was pretty worried about it and so my wife and I talked about it for quite a few weeks after that. We discussed a number of scenarios and none of them were ideal.

Where would we go? Who could we bring with us — besides our daughter? Can we live outside — just camping, hunting, fishing? Should we buy a bow and arrow and start practicing some basic archery? She even started to wonder about VERY simple survival skills like whether she could even build a fire from scratch, if she had to...

She also wanted to know specifically — and for the first time — what skills I actually had related to this. (It was the first time we really discussed any of my past military training and experiences.) My pretty standard Fort Benning boot camp, advanced training, and military service overseas calmed her fears a little. "But that was a long time ago" I said.

Honestly we all have worries like this... most are hidden *very* deep below the surface. But we fear the unexpected... and we fear change. And maybe most of all, we all fear the idea of losing control.

Understand that my wife is kind of a country girl, raised around horses all her life, rarely wears makeup (she's a natural beauty!), never uses an electric hair-dryer, and is not really a stranger to the outdoors. She doesn't even have a smartphone (I do!) — so to have this conversation with her is pretty interesting. But for all the people in our society who DO use a hair-dryer, microwave, play video games, carry a tablet, and use a search engine EVERY minute of every day — it's a radical idea to imagine all of us without any power.

So that's just fiction... Entertaining fiction nonetheless, but just fiction. Right? That could never happen... Right?

Well... it gets me to the idea for this short book. Here's a list — pulled together as a writer, educator, veteran, and U.S. citizen — of what I think are America's 10 Greatest Domestic Fears. But please understand, this is not meant to be an academic book, otherwise I would not use a pen name and would brag about it at work.

It's not a treatise on the state of terrorism in our world. It's not a statistical look at pandemic threats and where they might develop. It's not a study on the racial tensions in America or an economist's look at the class warfare issues that run from Wall Street to Main Street. I am not an expert on potable water, expounding on how we might manage food and water shortages in our country.

Nope. This book is for everyone in this country to understand the complex challenges and dangers that exist in our modern world. And these are the greatest fears that could change the domestic landscape of this country forever.

But this book is not meant to *scare* or alarm anyone... hopefully.

If anything, I truly believe that because knowledge is power, if we actually start to open a national discussion about these "fears," then the chance of them actually happening greatly diminishes.

And I'm smart enough to believe that many really, really intelligent and influential people are aware of these fears and are working on their prevention every single hour of every day.

INSPIRATION FOR FICTION

Maybe, this could also just be an idea book for *your* next post-apocalyptic science-fiction book, movie, video game, or TV series. Just make sure you send me a cut of the royalties...

So read this book and imagine the unimaginable, and make it the core of your next piece of fiction — then we'll ignite the discussion that way. If global power outages could so easily turn to toppled governments and warring republics in the "Revolution" story, and that gets people to seriously think about our electric grid and our infrastructure, then it served a purpose beyond sheer entertainment.

(Plus, I can imagine that what scares us all in fiction could also unite us in new ways... but I'll discuss that more later.)

RANKING

First a couple things about the overall organization of this book.

There are ten chapters in total of our greatest (and/or "worse") fears, starting immediately after this introduction chapter, and then followed by a brief "final thoughts" chapter. As much as the fears listed are pretty bad, there is no particular order to the way they are presented and they likely could have been presented here in almost *any* order. And as you might imagine, there is also a fair amount of overlap among these ten fears because many of these concepts do actually relate and interrelate to each other.

As I said, I believe that increased awareness of domestic *fears* like these, will *help* us to prevent them.

So let's begin with a brief look at domestic terrorism...

* * *

Chapter 1
Domestic Terrorism

There's no other way to describe it, but we still fear DOMESTIC TERRORISM in a very serious way in this country. Of course since 9/11, the United States has actually been quite nervous of the possibility of another such event on our soil. It's clearly one of the reasons that many citizens have supported our war efforts overseas. The idea that if our soldiers can stop "radical" individuals or groups in a far off land, then maybe we can avoid any acts of terrorism at home.

By definition because "terrorism" is meant to 'terrorize", Americans know that we've been lucky in his country NOT to have to deal with the regular suicide bombers, roadside bombs, and car bombs, and other attacks that many places around the globe have to endure on a regular basis. People around the world are routinely kept nervous and on edge by the constant threat of indiscriminate violence from terrorists making a statement.

Terrorism is effective because it does terrorize societies. That's why we fear it so much. We do not want to feel constantly afraid.

It's one of the reasons why the Boston Marathon bombing in 2013 was so shocking. It makes us feel unbelievably vulnerable and out of control to realize that we can have attacks happen on a busy street near a marathon finish line, even while surrounded by crowds of people, security, media, and police.

Many Americans also fear terrorist reprisals from foreign nationals who would visit this country to *bring* us a version of the violence that their home countries experience on a daily basis. What we've witnessed time and again is that people can become "radicalized" and changed in such a way that hurting, maiming, or killing innocent people doesn't matter to them any more.

We fear domestic terrorism for all of these reasons, and because as much as we try it's possible that we may never really understand the motives of the terrorists.

But one concern for our country that provides a possibly greater threat to our safety, is that many radicalized individuals may already be here on our soil, and may even be legal U.S. citizens. Terrorism by American citizens could create a new level of fear, distrust, and nationalism that could ignite other problems for our country. This explains the wiretap protocols in this country because as the Marathon bombings in Boston proved, the two terrorists had lived in this country for eleven years, one even attending an American university.

Next up, let's talk about the grocery store and our fears of shortages...

Chapter 2
Food Shortages

For as long as I can remember, I've known a couple people who actively stockpile food. I'm not talking about a few extra canned goods for hurricane season or to prepare for a long cold winter, but the idea that if anything actually really goes bad — they can eat for a while without worrying. They have lots of food — probably enough for all of their friends and relatives and for an extended period of time.

Maybe this kind of survivalist attitude is less common. It's a sort of Y2K, end-of-the-world, militia-type outlook on what could happen to all of our grocery stores that are filled with aisle after aisle of abundant food products.

Americans not only can go to any store and by cereal or bread or milk or soup — but can often choose between hundreds of varieties even in a suburban store!

But real food shortage is the next great American domestic fear. If you see how people react when a hurricane, winter storm, or tornado is coming and they find semi-depleted shelves at the grocery store — there's already an undertone of panic.

The problem with our food consumption in this country is that — in addition to eating a lot of it — we tend to shop on a pretty regular basis. As much as it's a total waste of gas and can be a waste of time — some people shop almost daily — and not just for *fresh* items like bakery items, fish, dairy, and more. We sort of expect that when we go to the store that we'll have a huge variety of choices of literally *every* product. Why else would we go on Saturday for the one item we forgot to buy on Thursday?

But what would happen if all the stores in our region were low on food? Could this even happen? (Remember any trucking strikes?)

This country would not do well with USSR-style bread lines or some sort of wide-scale food rationing. And whether or not the likelihood of food shortages happening in a major way is rare, just look at the aftermath of Hurricane Katrina in New Orleans and surrounding areas in 2005 to see how quickly conditions can change.

Sure we have many stores all over the country that carry a wide array food items— from convenience stores to big box retailers and discount wholesale clubs, but since many people only keep short-term quantities on hand at home - this could be develop into a problem relatively fast.

Of course, now this makes us want to stockpile at least a few months worth of non-perishables in the shed and basement. Last season's power outages and snow storms make you realize how vulnerable we really are.

Next serious domestic fear for Americans... biohazards.

Chapter 3
Biohazards:
Nuclear, Biological,
and Chemical

If you've ever seen images from (or visited) Hiroshima or Nagasaki, you know WHY there is a great fear in the American psyche of the hazards of nuclear, biological, or chemical warfare.

It might seem like the horrors of films rather than a reality, but because these weapons of mass destruction exist — and we don't always seem to know where they are — it's actually quite nerve-wracking.

The idea of exploding the power of the sun on the surface of our planet, makes nuclear weaponry so frightening, but the aftermath of radiation poisoning, other illnesses, and the threat of birth defects makes this an unimaginable horror.

Then when you consider the possibility of a rogue agent delivering some kind of toxic gas, biological or nerve agent on American soil — it's downright ridiculously scary. And how many local law enforcement authorities could detect many of the agents that are colorless, odorless, and tasteless...

This is perhaps the big problem with going to war against another country for a long time. Our national fear is that we can create an enemy or adversary who is so completely transformed by their need to strike back at the powerful United States, and when combined with a feeling of "nothing left to lose," it can be a tragic combination for all of us.

The "cold war" taught us that neither side really wanted mutual destruction, but does everyone feel that way?

This is why all of the political wrangling over the whereabouts of chemical and biological weapons. It's just inhuman to think of a foe pouring a compound that just melts off the skin or worse — in response to conventional warfare, which is bad enough... even when we deem it necessary.

Weaponized pathogens and infectious diseases pose an incredible global risk as well because of the difficulty in tracking and securing the materials, substances, and organisms involved.

Now let's talk about a very precious commodity we can't live without...

Chapter 4
Water Shortages & Drought

Whether it's through widespread droughts, intentional or unintentional contamination or other by means, many of us fear a real shortage of water in this country.

More and more we read about the scarcity of fresh drinking water — and the control over it — being the cause or underlying cause of conflicts in different regions around the globe.

Drinkable water is a really difficult commodity to replace if your own water becomes contaminated or just goes away due to extended droughts. Of course, it also affects food production because if we ever did have a serious water shortage in this country, then our agricultural, cattle, and poultry output would be greatly diminished. It could lead to a deepening spiral of food and water issues.

Of course, the area which concerns us the most — especially in region where there does not seem to be a shortage of seasonal rain — is the idea of a water-supply that it contaminated or poisoned for some reason — either through natural, accidental, or terrorist means.

If the major drinking water sources for an urban area were suddenly unavailable, the demands for bottled water would overwhelm supply without a huge activation of resources.

Water is an unbelievably precious commodity that has even slowly taken its place on Wall Street as institutional investors can imagine a time where it's as precious as oil, gold, or silver. And since we need it to survive, I would argue that oil, gold, and silver mean much less — if you don't agree ask a thirsty person.

Now let's talk about the fear of a domestic civil war...

Chapter 5
Civil War

I don't know about you, but I think that in many ways this country is an amazing feat of both political and social engineering. It's amazing that we have so many people, so many ideas, so many different sub-cultures, and yet we remain united as a single country. It's great and it's inspiring to others around the globe.

But each time we approach a major election, or have a major social conflict, I start to hear citizens from around the country talk in a very contentious manner about all our differences. It makes me have a sense of some of the divisions in this country that run actually deep. But what I think keeps those divisions in check is that most citizens would never want to see us ever split up this country into any smaller parts, and we'd never want to see us break down into some kind of CIVIL WAR again.

The thought is almost unimaginable until you look around the world and you see plenty of examples of regions that have broken in two — or worse — shattered into many pieces while the citizens fight in some kind a brutal civil war.

Could it happen here? Hopefully not.

But there are a number of other American domestic fears spelled out in this short book which could be that small spark of a civil war, but keeping this from ever happening (again) on our soil must really keep some people up late at night. (Keep working folks!)

And for those doubters... in the former Yugoslavia, it only took a few short years (1989-1992) for that country to break up and then over the next few years be replaced by five new states (including Bosnia, Kosovo, and Serbia). That transition was violent, bloody, and involved thousands of casualties. I'm sure they were just as surprised as well when their society changed...

Since this fear is about an internal 'civil' war — notice that I didn't say we would actually fear an outside war or attack on our soil. That's because I believe that there is so much national pride about our borders that I think — like the story lines in films like "Red Dawn" (old or new version), or the sci-fi Independence Day — we would be galvanized as a people if this country was ever invaded. That's why I don't count that among our top ten greatest fears... We would likely become so unbelievably united in a way that we haven't seen in this country since the second world war

Next to concerns about urban rioting...

Chapter 6
Urban Rioting

Every police department in every major city in our country has riot gear. It's true. Law enforcement officials know that large crowds that have the possibility of changing into an angry "mob" can be a very dangerous situation on the ground. Generally, when you see police officers and emergency response tactical teams in riot gear on the evening news, it's generally to disperse a crowd before that can even develop.

But luckily, large-scale rioting in our cities is a relatively rare occurrence, but it's definitely among the major fears of our citizens - not only that of law enforcement.

Most of what we know about urban riots in this country seems to refer back to the 1960's, but if you look at the 1992 Los Angeles riots (after the Rodney King trial), and a number of other protests in recent years, you realize that tensions can escalate quickly and these crowds do often get out of control.

Recently with the St. Louis-area riots (yes, Ferguson is a suburb), we realize that this is actually a big concern for America. That's why it captured headlines for so long.

As Americans, we don't want to even imagine the widespread societal impact if our streets became regularly violent. Would schools close? Businesses? Would travel and tourism stop? Would the stock market drop (or worse, crash!), and then our local and regional economies collapse?

Would the localized violence then turn into a larger problem? What can happen is that the media's attention of localized urban riots can often 'radicalize' others across the country towards more widespread action. Then it snowballs... Mass rioting could ensue across our country, and that would radically change our day-to-day way of life — but that's an overarching concern outlined in a later chapter.

Historically, examples of extreme urban violence in this country are connected to our civil rights movement — the fear today is also that any urban rioting could also be racially motivated, and could lead the country towards a dangerous battle over our economic and social inequalities — many of which seem to unfairly straddle the color lines in our society.

We fear urban rioting because it would be disruptive, dangerous, and could lead to drastic changes in our freedom of movement, congregation, and more — with increased police or military presence on our streets, curfews, and even the move towards martial law in some places. Pretty frightening stuff for our democratic nation.

Next up, let's talk about the class divides in our society which also makes many worry...

Chapter 7
Class Warfare:
Lower vs. Upper

The Occupy Wall Street movement, which started in 2011 and may not have officially ended, signaled the tip-of-the-iceberg of an undeclared class warfare problem in this country.

Whether the lower or middle class will ever rise up against the upper class and ultra-elite in this country remains to be seen, but the tensions are obviously there. Since it was Wall Street's greed combined with an overly-aggressive real estate industry, combined with shady consumers who exaggerated their ability to repay loans which caused our 2008 great recession, many are still mad that "regular" Americans paid the price while the bailouts saved many wealthy citizens.

The economic divide is a big problem in this country and real class warfare — I'm sure — scares every millionaire and billionaire... especially those whose fortune was not made due to innovation, hard work, or the spirit of entrepreneurship. Many wealthy Americans protect their riches because they know it comes from loopholes, mistakes, inequalities, or problems in our society - rather than one the perpetuates the American dream.

This magical, inviting country where dreams can happen means that any small town athlete can be discovered, tossed into the spotlight, and receive a $10 million sports contract, or some young actress — a few years into her career — can earn that kind of salary for a single film. But with many, many U.S. citizens living in poverty, or actually homeless, a fair amount of the security expenditures among the rich and famous is really about protecting themselves from any personal threats, as well as threats related to class warfare and/or backlash over the economic inequalities.

Don't get me wrong — our land of opportunity and entrepreneurship is truly amazing, and I wouldn't want to live anywhere else in the world, but I'm still more in the middle-zone of this economic ladder. That said, I definitely don't want to see our society *implode* because the poor start to strike out at the rich.

Our country prides itself on being a place where this entrepreneurial spirit, unbridled hard work, and determination can lead to the "American Dream," but many people feel economically and socially held back from even participating in this country's best opportunities. (The digital divide is one example — so if you have no access to the internet or the world wide web, then this is a very different country for you and your family!)

Of course, this issue can also relate to our fears around urban rioting, and could also be linked with other concerns if we see any widespread shortages of food or water in the United States.

Now let's talk about disease, and outbreaks...

Chapter 8
Disease, Outbreaks, and Epidemics

The current tensions surrounding the global spread of Ebola underscore how afraid our citizens really are about disease, outbreaks, and epidemics. Whether it's Avian Flu, SARS, H1N1, Ebola, or whatever virus becomes the imminent crisis of the season, Americans worry about how our huge melting pot of people and relatively open borders could lead to some disaster stemming from a fast-moving, contagious virus.

Sure it's the stuff of movies, but with international airports in nearly every major city in the country and the possibility of nearly anyone spreading a deadly disease inside our borders, that's why every effort is made to calm the public about outbreaks.

Public places all around our country including department stores, shopping malls, schools/colleges, and even sporting events would immediately become abandoned for fear of being around other people as a virus is spreading.

The pandemic fear also affects our equity markets, because recent announcements of new Ebola cases identified in the United States were blamed for major pullbacks in the Dow, Nasdaq, and S&P on those trading days. We can only imagine the impact it would have if there was a serious outbreak— not only restricting travel — but creating a widespread sense of fear and panic.

What would shut down? The real issue is the complete fragility of our infrastructure to risks like this.

And since symptoms like high fever, vomiting, and diarrhea can be caused by a number of sources — many of which are NOT deadly viruses — it's also possible for any reported outbreak, epidemic, or PANDEMIC to turn into an uncontrollable level of hysteria which could lead to even bigger problems in our society.

Scary.

Now let's discuss our quality of life...

Chapter 9
Radical Changes in Quality of Life

Again, without implying that any of these fears presented here are in a particular order — there is a common thread among them in this final fear.

What Americans likely fear most is something that would radically change the quality of life for many in this country. As I mentioned before, this is one of those fears that combines so many of the others - but also opens the discussion up to fears and threats not even contemplated here.

When 9/11 occurred, immediate changes were made in our intelligence community and national security — rightly so — which made changes to all of our lives. There has been great debate in recent years whether or not we traded too much of our country's freedom for a greater sense of security. That debate is *beyond* this little book, but I will say that life in America clearly changed.

With another major act of domestic terrorism, some biological/chemical warfare attack, or widespread food and water shortages — life in this country would change overnight. It's even possible that these could be the shifts that bring about class warfare, urban rioting, or even a civil war on our soil.

What we fear most is that our way of lives — as Americans — with our hopes, our dreams, our jobs, our families, and our futures — would all disappear.

Who wants to wake up one day and find out that everything is gone or everything is different — and now life is about pure survival, and holding on to whatever humanity we have left.

That's what we most fear.

Final Thoughts

As a family man with a young daughter, let me say that all of these American fears scare the crap out of me — and hopefully you too. I want nothing more than a wonderfully safe, productive, and happy country for all our children to grow up, so hopefully everyone reading this takes the knowledge and awareness of these threats and helps makes sure that these things can never come to pass.

At the beginning when I mentioned that this all started with a TV series, I encourage authors, novelists, filmmakers, screenwriters, songwriters, poets, painters, and others to embrace this list of fears and help us understand why they should be reflected upon, and then actively prevented all across the globe — not just here at home. This is where storytelling is a very powerful tool.

Our awareness of our own fears nationally should also lead us to help others around the planet combat this same list in their own little corner of the globe, in an attempt to preserve their humanity and to provide a better planet for their children as well as ours. If we stem outbreaks elsewhere, we can prevent pandemics on our soil. If we help to preserve and protect global drinking water supplies, we can help prevent rioting due to conflicts over basic resources.

These problems are so interconnected, but they are all avoidable.

Best of luck to us all, and thanks for reading this.

* * *

About the Author

Derek G. America is a the pen name for an American writer and educator - who also happens to be a veteran who served his country in Iraq, Saudi Arabia, and Kuwait. He currently lives in New England with his wife and daughter.

***Please consider leaving a review wherever you got this book, because most people don't, and it helps more readers find this book. Thank you.

* * *

Other recent books by Derek G. America

You Can Be Rich Without Being a Scumbag

Server Server

and a series of notebooks and journals.

www.ingramcontent.com/pod-product-compliance
Lightning Source LLC
Chambersburg PA
CBHW030548290526
45786CB00004B/1923